As I Recall...

Farm kid recollections from the 'fifties

Joel Lovstad

To Jeff —
Enjoy!

Joel Lovstad 8/20/2016

Lovstad Publishing
Poynette, Wisconsin
Lovstadpublishing@live.com

ISBN: 0615787304
ISBN-13: 978-0615787305

Printed in the United States of America

Cover design by Lovstad Publishing
Cover photo: Author Joel Lovstad, age 8,
with his trusty companion, Snooker, 1956.

This little book is dedicated to my family,
for all the fond memories they helped to create
on that Wisconsin farm where I grew up.

CONTENTS

As I Recall...

As I Recall...

We lived on a small farm that was nearly at the end of a township road. There was only one more place beyond ours, and if that road ever had a name or designated number at that time, I never knew of it. The road surface was gravel then, disgustingly dusty in the summertime, slippery and treacherous and often snow-blocked in the winter, and nearly impassable because of mud during the spring thaws. Once you made it out of our valley, there were a number of alternate routes into town or to the main highway, but generally, they all rendered about the same conditions when the conditions were at their worst. Just getting to town, sometimes, involved a major undertaking that not only taxed the vehicle and tested the skills of the driver, but often brought out an inner character that made going to church the following Sunday more necessary – IF you could get there.

My folks bought that place and moved there before I came into the world, and that little farm was my universe during my childhood – the only place I had ever known as "home," and I was still calling it that even after I went off to college, the military, and the pursuit of a career. That plot of land in Wisconsin holds some fond memories for me, but whether or not my early life there influenced the shape of my life in later years, I cannot rightly say, as my father never tried to persuade me to follow in his agricultural footsteps, even though that was the only life he had ever known. Perhaps he thought there were better ways to live in the world, and there was a time in my life when I believed that, too. But in all honesty, I doubt that I have ever found it.

This is not meant to be the story of my life, but rather, just observations of the bits and pieces from my youth, and recollections of life "down on the farm"... as I recall.

First Memories

The yard was my kingdom when I was very small. It figures into all of my earliest memories. The castle was the old log house with its additions and white slate siding. It had an open porch across the front with lathe-turned pillars holding up the roof. There was no railing, but the deck of the porch was quite close to the ground, and so there was little danger of a fall resulting in serious injury. That porch was enclosed with walls and windows later on, and it made for a dandy place to be when the weather didn't allow me to play outside.

In the world of the yard surrounding our farmhouse grew several giant white pines. There were no branches low enough to temp a boy to climb, but that was okay. As time went on, I discovered plenty of other trees nearby for that purpose. The huge pines in the yard stood as mighty sentinels, always guarding, always protecting, always giving generous and pleasant shade over most of the lawn. And there was the huge garden where my mother worked her magic from early spring until late fall. A steep hillside rose from the outer edge of the garden to the roadway above, and fencing around the rest of the yard reduced my attempts of escape until I was old enough when any kind of restraint was no longer effective.

Mom hung the laundry to dry on the clothesline in the back yard, and that's where I had my sand pile. There were raspberry bushes along the fence, and in the far corner was a rhubarb patch. And on an elm tree, there in the back yard, hung a wren house. I remember a pair of wrens occupying that little house every spring for as long as we lived on the farm. I believe it was the same family to return every year, for when they arrived, it seemed as though they would let us know they had returned safely from their winter quarters by singing gaily outside our windows, and then they would busily begin to set up housekeeping in that little house that they knew would be waiting for them. We were always thrilled to have them back.

Right in front of the house was a cistern with a cast iron pump. I just barely remember a smaller version of that pump in our kitchen before we had "pressurized" water, and the cistern was the source of the water we used in the house. The cistern and its pump still remained useful in later times, as it provided the water for washing the field dirt off hands and faces before going into the house for a meal. And it was always a good place for a cool drink on a hot summer day.

Just beyond the cistern stood a rickety old building about ten feet by twenty feet. It had once been a summer kitchen, but all I remember it to be was a catchall for junk.

Dad finally tore it down and hauled away all the junk, and the square of weed free, grassless, rich, black soil became one of Mom's prized flower gardens. It already had very productive lilac trees around it.

It was largely a world of play then, as it is with most children today, although the store toys were few. My outdoor sand pile saw a toy farm tractor or two, and a couple of dump trucks, but most of the tools of play were things like an old barn door hinge, a broken cement trowel, and discarded kitchen utensils. Store toys were reserved for indoors when it rained.

My brother was nearly six years older, usually off somewhere with Dad learning farm stuff, and my sister was grown and had ventured somewhere far away to work, so I spent a great deal of time alone in that yard. Even without siblings or other neighbor kids as playmates, it wasn't so bad. I don't recall any thoughts of loneliness. The barn cats could always be persuaded to romp in the grass on the lawn, and that was exceptionally fun when they brought a batch of kittens along. I remember the cats as great playtime companions.

There were so many curious, fascinating things to keep me occupied. The two crabapple trees on the far side of the lawn by the granary blossomed in a flurry of white, and the lilacs cast an unforgettable fragrance about the yard. Every now and then a wild rabbit scurried into the garden in search of a lunch, but when I tried to get near, he would be gone quicker than I could say "bunny!" And I always liked to watch the cows in the pasture behind the house, lazily roaming and chomping on grass next to the creek. It was fascinating that all those little birds hopped around on the ground among those big cows, and neither the cows nor the birds seemed concerned with the presence of the other. I thought they must have been really good friends.

And the creek – there was another mysterious place that I viewed from behind the barrier of the fence. It meandered through our valley, shaded here and there by clumps of willow trees, and played host to a pair of whooping cranes that came every spring and stayed all summer. I could hear the frogs and the gurgling and I could see the sparkling water rushing over the rocks, and I so wanted to be right there with it, but it would be a couple more years before I could claim that new territory as part of my domain.

Exactly when that magical time came about would be difficult to pinpoint, but eventually I was permitted to tag along with my older brother on countless missions of exploration and discovery, and it wasn't long until I knew where all the creek crossings were, and where all the cow paths led through the hills and woods. And then it wasn't long until I was riding my imaginary stallion, driving my imaginary stagecoach, and fighting thousands of imaginary savage Indians. The center of my universe had moved from the porch to the granary that was now whatever my imagination conjured it up to be. It was a general store, an army fort, a blacksmith shop, the sheriff's office and jail, the stagecoach stop, a feed mill, and I think it may have been the railroad depot a time or two, and even the James Gang hideout, and a hundred other things that I don't recall.

The granary was a storehouse of treasures. Not only did it hold bins of oats and corn; it served as Dad's workshop where he kept all his tools above, on, and under a wooden bench, and on shelves were bags of nails of all sizes, tin cans full of nuts and bolts and screws, and boxes of other assorted hardware items. It was where Mom kept all her gardening tools and supplies, and where we stored the sacks of cow and chicken feed that we brought back from the mill. The upstairs loft stored all the unused and forgotten tools of more primitive farming days, and parts of obsolete machinery, furniture, housewares, and hundreds of other items, all of which would send a present-day antique dealer into cartwheels. It's no wonder that a young boy with a good imagination could create his own little world in that old building.

Now that I was old enough to be venturing out of the yard on my own, I was old enough to start assuming chores, too. The first one I recall was retrieving the mail. In the middle of those long childhood days, I was always excited to see a dust cloud up on the road, and soon a car would come down the hill behind the barn. By the time I had raced to the end of the driveway, I heard the rumble of the bridge planks, and Howard, the mailman was turning around and pulling up to deposit the mail in the boxes mounted on the bridge railing. Howard always had a big smile and a friendly wave for me.

Some days there'd only be the daily newspaper – the La Crosse Tribune, and once a week, the Westby Times. The overabundance of advertising and junk mail that floods the mail nowadays was practically nonexistent then. Red-letter days at that time were marked with the arrival of the J.C. Penny's, Sears & Roebuck, or Montgomery-Ward seasonal catalogs. And of course, Mom got her monthly Ladies' Home Journal and Dad kept up with the latest farm news in the Wisconsin Agriculturist.

By the time I arrived at the house, Mom was setting the table, and Dad was usually there too, a little early for dinner. That gave him a little extra time to scan the paper before eating, and then afterwards, he'd really get serious about reading the articles.

Hard as I tried, sometimes, to keep all that play energy flowing, the living room sofa lured me with little effort, and I drifted into a nap. Even though I probably didn't intend to go to sleep, I didn't mind that little mid-day siesta, either.

The old granary is one of only four original structures remaining on the farm where I grew up. It is very possibly the first building constructed on the 1800s homestead, where the family lived while a log house was being built. That house still remains, too, although it has seen extensive remodeling and several additions over the years, and has no outward appearances of its original log form. This photo was taken before recent restoration.

"Okay. I'll drive...you read the map." My late cousin, Alan and I going for a ride in the Radio Flyer around the back yard.

SPRING

From that first really warm day of spring until the corn and oats were planted, time on the farm had an air of bustle about it. These were the days of change. The ditches and gullies ran full with snowmelt and the creek started overflowing its banks. At first, the trees that had stood stark and naked against the sky were tinged with a faint green lace, and then almost overnight, they seemed to explode into an ocean of rich, verdant foliage. Sweet smelling blossoms sprinkled the apple trees in the little orchard on the north hill, and I could almost feel the pulse of things growing.

Dad mended fences that, somehow, always seemed to deteriorate over the winter. It was indeed a lot of fun riding on the trailer loaded with fence posts, spools of barbed wire, a bucket of staples, and all the necessary tools, as Dad drove over the hills and through the woods – the places that at no other time were ever navigated with tractor and trailer. When we returned to the house about noon, we'd find Mom churning and smoothing the soil in the flowerbeds around the yard, preparing for a day of planting. But there would be a hearty meal waiting on the kitchen table, too.

After we ate our dinner, it was out to the other side of the farm to check all the fences there. When Dad was satisfied that the cows would be contained, we'd let them out of the barn and chase them toward the grassy pastures. This was not new territory for them, but they'd always be hesitant at first, after being cooped up in the barn all winter. Once they got out into the fresh air, though, they were like a bunch of children on the last day of school, romping about and bunting each other, and of course, sniffing curiously at everything in sight. Eventually, they'd find their way to the green pastures along the creek bank. There they set to cropping the new grass furiously, as if they had been the victims of starvation all winter.

Like a ladies' auxiliary, a heard of cows had one poke-and-snoop character – the matriarch – the self-appointed leader. When she decided it was time to move on, the rest followed, and usually by the end of that first day of freedom, the herd had sampled grass from nearly every accessible corner of their pasture empire.

One sure sign of spring came when the trays of all sorts of budding or blooming flowers and the big wire racks containing packets of every imaginable variety of garden seeds appeared on the sidewalk in front of the grocery stores in town. In our small town, there was no greenhouse or lawn and garden center; the grocers carried and displayed a fairly good selection of plants and seeds, and the hardware store maintained a supply of just about everything else one might need in the garden.

The regular grocery-shopping trip on at least one early spring Saturday became the all-important garden seed mission as well. Every member of the family got involved with the garden, and it all started as we gathered around the sidewalk racks selecting just the right vegetable seeds to plant. We usually stuck with the old standbys – green beans, peas, carrots, beets, radishes, cucumbers, lettuce, onions, and sweet corn – lots of sweet corn – pumpkins

and squash, and then there was always picking out a dozen each of tomato and cabbage plants, already started in little cardboard pots. Mom would choose a bunch of potted flowers, some with blossoms and some without, for planting in the beds along the house walls – pansies, petunias, daisies, and always geraniums. By the time we headed for home, the car looked like a rolling greenhouse.
Mom really had a way with flowers, and when it came to the vegetable garden, she had two green thumbs. But it wasn't all her doing – we all took part in the success of the garden, and rightly so, as it provided a large portion of the meals we ate all the next winter.

After Dad plowed and worked the garden plot with the tractor, we all went to work with rakes and hoes to prepare the soil. Then the rows were carefully staked out and the planting began. Dad reserved a large area for potatoes, and Mom reserved a strip along the edge – sort of a buffer zone next to the lawn for her flowers. It was an all-day family project, and everyone seemed to enjoy it.

My most notable gardening experience occurred at about age nine. A couple of years earlier, Mom planted a modest row of poppies in her flower section. They bloomed gloriously and added a nice bit of red and yellow color to the edge of the lawn. That fall, when everything turned brown, I learned about the seedpods at the top of the poppy stems left standing leafless in the rows. Dad explained that if I cut off the pods and let them dry, the pods could be broken open and the seeds inside could be planted the next spring. I followed his instructions, and the next spring, I planted a row of poppy seeds along the entire length of the garden. By mid-summer, there bloomed an impressive row of poppies. I was so proud of my accomplishment that I saw fit to harvest the seeds again that fall. This harvest rendered two or three quart jars of seed after the pods were opened. Unbeknownst to anyone else, I planted some "extra" poppy seed the next spring. Mom seemed a little upset with me when poppies started growing everywhere, and especially when they dominated her usual flower section of the main garden. But if ever there was a more spectacular array of hybrid poppies in colors unimaginable, it certainly wasn't in our neighborhood. Our garden that year was completely engulfed by a sea of fabulous color. When the word got out, people from miles around made special trips by our farm just to see my wonderful poppy field.

That year I received strict orders not to harvest any more poppy seeds.

The Geese Are Coming...
It Must Be Spring!

We had watched the shriveled, dry leaves drift to the ground on the fall's chilly winds. We had seen the animals scurrying about gathering the last bits of food for their winter supply, and had bundled ourselves, too, in a few extra layers of long johns and sweaters against winter's bitter grip. But now, the warm springtime breezes allowed us to shed the extra clothes. A veil of green shrouded the trees once again, and all the little creatures came scurrying out of their burrows after a long winter's nap, happy and curious of the fresh, new world.

I was always happy and curious with the springtime, too. It was a time to romp in the fresh air and to feel the warm sunshine on my back, and a time, once again, to reunite with nature.

Artists and photographers have always portrayed nature and its countless wonders on canvas and film for those who are not fortunate enough to experience it firsthand. But I was one of the lucky ones to grow up in its midst. Nature was all around me, and I only had to step out my front door! And the spring always offered so many new sights and adventures. Living in the country allowed me to be more aware.   Accounting for all the wild creatures living there – or, perhaps, just visiting our farm now and then – became a favorite activity.

Our farm was situated partly in a valley with a stream,

and partly on wooded hills. It provided various forms of habitat that attracted a wide variety of birds. Every year the swallows returned to their nesting places in the barns and sheds, and a family of wrens took up residency in the little birdhouse nailed to the trunk of an elm tree in our back yard. Cardinals loved our big pine trees, and the robins found their daily feast of earthworms on our big, grassy lawn. Bluebirds and finches seemed to like the open fields up on the hills; diving kingfishers kept watch from the willows along the creek for minnows and tadpoles, and English sparrows and chickadees – well, they were everywhere. A pair of mysterious whooping cranes made their home somewhere along the creek bank for the summer, and a few wood ducks and mallards would visit the valley stream from time to time.

But the most intriguing of all our winged friends were the geese. In our valley, their numbers were not many, and their stays were brief. Perhaps our farm was merely a rest stop for those few amid their long journey to who-knows-where.

The southbound November geese never stopped, but passed over in their high altitude formations, as if they thought there might be guns awaiting their arrival, as was the case on most ponds and marshes at that time of year. They would have been safe in our valley, but I guess they didn't know that.

The April geese, though, were different. They announced the season's change with their noisy chatter, flying lower and in smaller flocks. A few would circle overhead for a while, probably surveying the prospects of food and lodging, and then they'd come sailing down like falling oak leaves on a breeze, spread their landing gear, and glide gracefully onto the wide pools of the creek. Once they touched down, they put up a honking and splashing that shook any remaining hints of winter from last year's brown and brittle cattails.

During their stay, these geese made daily trips to and from the nearby cornfields, picking their way through the stubble left from last year's crop. There, they feasted on the waste corn that the snow had kept covered all winter, and that the crows, rabbits, and field mice had not yet found. Then, in the evening, they would retreat to the stream again, carrying on with the jabbering and splashing until the night shadows fell upon them. A few days later, they soared away, not to return again until after the next spring floods.

If I could have understood any of their babbling, perhaps I would have learned where these geese were going, and where they had been all winter. But I couldn't, and it is just as well that their journey remained a mystery.

Crops and Cows and Chickens

Spending my boyhood on a farm, I developed – from my father – the habit of examining the state of crops wherever I go. He was a man who loved farming, and to hear him talk of silage and oats and rye grass was a cure for all the ailments of mankind. He would often stop the car when we were driving about, and sometimes even walk to the edge of a field and contemplate on the way the crop was growing, or sometimes to watch another farmer operating machinery, either because of intrigue, or, maybe unfamiliarity. He did this whether we were in our own neighborhood, or out for a Sunday sightseeing excursion in Minnesota or Iowa, or wherever we might be.

The growing green things he loved, and toward animals he showed great affection and respect. On our farm, we kept cows and chickens as the only livestock – no pigs, sheep, or goats. He cared for them as if they were all his pets, and they loved him for that. He could walk into the pasture of the grazing animals and in a moment be the center of a herd of mooing, adoring cows, and he could approach nearly any one of them and scratch their necks and rub under their chins.

Those cows, of course, were the lifeblood of our farm, for it was the milk they produced that generated the majority of my dad's regular income. So it is no wonder why he made special effort to see that they were well cared for and happy. All the crops raised on our farm were for the purpose of feeding the livestock, and only after a bumper crop was any grain or hay sold to market.

For many years, though, our farm produced another commodity – eggs. My earliest recollections of that were of my mother trading crates of eggs for groceries at the various small stores in our town. As I recall, there were usually more eggs than any one store would take, so it often meant two or three stops at different stores.

But then, as progress marched on and the markets reached out from the bigger cities, it became more convenient to sell the product, as the wholesalers started sending trucks to the farms to pick up the eggs, and it was no longer necessary for Mom and Dad to haul them to town in search of a buyer. It also meant the opportunity for a larger, more profitable operation.

So it became a yearly ritual – every spring we'd clean and scrub the little brooder house, lay in a clean, dry bed of straw, and rig up several heat lamps that hung just a couple of feet from the floor. Then it was a matter of waiting for Ed Storbakken who ran the hatchery to tell us the chicks were hatching. This was always an exciting time for me. I loved going to the hatchery and peeking in the incubator windows and seeing the baby chicks breaking out from their shells. A few days later, we would go to the hatchery again, but this time we would carry home several big, flat cardboard boxes containing two or three hundred of the fuzzy little yellow chicks. Within a short while, the floor of the brooder house was a scurrying mass of yellow as the chicks darted about and crowded under the warmth of the heat lamps.

As I grew a little older – and big enough to carry a feed pail – it became one of my daily chores to help care for the chicks. Of course, as a youngster I found it great fun rather than a chore to spend long hours among those playful, curious little creatures. They would dart about the brooder house floor, and every once in a while, one would try to fly with its tiny, immature wings, only to tumble into an awkward, fluttering yellow heap. And it always seemed to amuse the rest of the flock, as a chorus of peep, peep, peeps filled the house.

As the weeks flew by, the fuzzy little chicks grew quite rapidly. Their soft yellow down transformed into tarnished-looking feathers, that in time turned to a brilliant white. Their peep, peeps changed to chirp, chirps, to cluck, clucks. There were usually three or four roosters in the crowd, and by the time they were a few weeks old, they were making feeble attempts at crowing – with little success. But in time, and with practice, their scratchy little er-er-errrrs became more pronounced, and they were cock-a-doodle-doo-ing like old pros. They were making themselves heard, sometimes far too often, and they were sure to wake up the whole neighborhood at dawn.

Then came the day when the chicks had grown to adults, when they were moved into the chicken coop to spend the rest of their days. Now they had grown to know me as their food provider, and every time I entered the coop with pails of feed, they clustered around my feet in wild anticipation of a tasty meal of mash and shelled corn. Oh, how they loved their shelled corn!

As I recall, I was about seven or eight years old, and by then I was tagging along with my dad when he helped the neighbors with big jobs such as haying or corn harvest. In return, they would help my dad with his crops. But as just a little guy like me, I didn't always go out in the fields with the men. I was relegated to staying in the yard to seek whatever entertainment I could. The neighbors – the Sordahls, Otto and Ernest – were two brothers who had taken over the family farm operation after their father passed away. Their farm adjoined ours where they lived with their sister, Lydia, and their mother, Selma. And there were so many interesting things at their place to entertain a little boy.

One of the features of their farm that held my fascination was the flock of Bantam chickens – "Banties," we called them. This breed of chicken is smaller in size and comes in all sorts of brilliant mixed colors – especially the roosters – reds, blues, purples, greens, and everything in between. The hens were generally reddish-brown, black, or tan, and a little less flamboyant. I guess it was, perhaps, their unique and somewhat exotic appearance that intrigued me, and the fact that they were quite tame. I could pick them up and hold them, and they seemed to enjoy the attention.

Otto recognized my fondness of the Banties, and one day he asked me if I would like to have a pair of them to take home. I was elated, and when Dad said it was okay, I couldn't wait to introduce my new pets to the rest of our flock.

Naturally, pets must have names, and because they were the only brightly colored chickens on our farm, they weren't hard to pick out of the crowd! Their names became Otto and Lydia – perhaps the only chickens on our farm ever to have names.

But Otto and Lydia didn't care to socialize with the rest of our birds. Instead, they chose to roost in the hay barn at night, and they seemed contented to roam around the buildings by day, scavenging for food, rather than joining the White Rocks and Leghorns at the feed trough. Of course, I was always supplementing their diet with some shelled corn and oats whenever I saw them around the granary.

Now you might think that they were vulnerable to predators, roaming freely as they did, but I soon learned these little critters were quite feisty, and more than once I saw Otto chasing a cat or the dog away from his territory. No, they weren't so vulnerable, after all.

I did worry, though, the next spring when Lydia disappeared. She wasn't seen for quite some time, and I feared that she had fallen prey to a fox or some other wild animal. For days I searched the entire farm, hoping to find some trace, but nothing. Then, to my utter delight, she reappeared one day, with six baby chicks scurrying around her, and Otto strutting alongside making sure no harm would come to his new family.

On that day, I learned to never give up hope for something so meaningful as life.

Two more of the original buildings remaining on our farm have been restored and preserved by the current owners. Chicken coop (top[); Corn crib (below).

The old-fashioned side-delivery hay rake (top) was first designed to be drawn across the fields by horses. Note the seat mounted high at the front of the machine between the two drive wheels. That's where the operator sat while driving the horses. In later years, after the age of the gasoline engine tractors began to replace the "horse power," many of the farm implements such as this one would be converted and modified for use as tractor-drawn machinery. Because the mechanical operation of the machine depended on the rotation of its own large wheels, such a conversion was rather simple and inexpensive, making it a practical procedure for most farmers, and saving them the expense of buying new machinery.

Horse-drawn hay mowers (lower) were also commonly converted for use with gasoline tractors. Note the lugs on the steel wheels that provided good traction on grassy ground. Power from the rotation of the wheels is transmitted through a gearbox to operate the cutting bar sickle. The angled board mounted at the end of the cutting bar guided the cut hay away from the adjacent standing hay, thus keeping it from clogging the machine on the next pass across the field. The operator drove the horses while riding in the seat at the rear. Levers are within easy reach for raising or dropping the cutting bar to the ground, and for disengaging the gearbox to stop the sickle while the machine is maneuvered at the end of the field to align it for the next swath. The long beam at the front extends between the horses of a team and is attached to the harness. When converting the mower for tractor power, this beam was shortened considerably and modified for hitching to the tractor drawbar.

SUMMER

An *Allis-Chalmers* tractor had replaced the team of workhorses on our farm before any of my first-hand recollections of those early days. But much of the machinery we used for many years after the beginning of the tractor age was carried over from the "horsepower" era and was converted, adapted, modified, and redesigned in all ways necessary to render it useful and suitable at the drawbar of a gasoline engine tractor. This wasn't the practice just on our place – it was the common procedure on just about every farm in those days. Eventually, as the tractors got bigger and more powerful, and most farmers started feeling the need to accomplish more fieldwork in less time, much of the old horse-drawn machinery found the scrap iron pile, and the more modern, larger, stronger, more efficient, and brightly painted versions started adding their color to nearly every neighborhood field. But until that later transformation gradually occurred, fields were tilled and crops were planted and harvested with the tools once pulled by Molly and Dobbin.

The haying season lasted for most of the summer, and always seemed to constitute the major portion of the farm work, as far as the crops were concerned. Alfalfa, timothy, and clover grew fast, providing there was at least some rainfall, and it wasn't long between the time the last fields were cut and the hay in the barn, and when the first ones harvested were green again with a second crop. If the season was favorable, sometimes a third cutting could be accomplished.

Most of the manual labor has been eliminated now, but youngsters of today aren't experiencing the fun we had. There was a pleasant atmosphere and a special kind of personal satisfaction to haying back then that has vanished with the advent of so many mechanical aids.

There was, first of all, the steady clackety-clack of the mower as the little Allis-Chalmers purred along and the sickle blades methodically slashed through the alfalfa, timothy and aromatic clover. That mower was one of the modified implements from the earlier horse days. It had, like all the horse-drawn machines, one of those rounded, contoured steel seats for a rider, as that's where the operator sat while driving the horses. Behind a tractor, though, there wasn't much need for those seats anymore, but there wasn't any point in removing them either. And as long as they were there, it was a good place to ride, and great fun for a young boy.

Frequently, the small inhabitants of the hay field scampered out in mortal fright. Here and there a rabbit would go hippity hopping out of danger, and there was an occasional stop to move a bird's nest to the safety of the fence line. Field mice were beyond counting, but we were never too concerned about them. On rare occasions, we might scare up a red fox that had been hunting the smaller rodents, or a ground hog feasting on the succulent alfalfa leaves.

Words cannot describe the distinctive fragrance of freshly mowed hay, although many a poet has attempted it with countless written lines. There wasn't time for poetic thoughts while working in the hayfield, but when I was old enough to drive the tractor, I became very much aware of a sense of satisfaction as the cut alfalfa stems fell neatly behind the cutting bar in straight, orderly swaths. That same feeling followed me as I stopped under a shady tree for a cool drink of water from a mason jar wrapped up in a brown paper bag, and I surveyed the finished field.

Raking the hay into windrows after it had dried for a day or two, depending on the sunshine and humidity, was another of those "artistic" hayfield operations. I barely remember the dump rake that Dad first used, but it was one of the implements that rusted away under some oak trees out in the pasture when it was replaced by a "side delivery" rake. The new rake, too, had a seat for the driver of a team. A reel consisting of four long bars holding the tines rotated in the machine's framework in the opposite direction of ground travel, and "swept" the cut hay off to one side into neat windrows. The straighter the windrows, the better they were for loading.

The hay loader was another apparatus that soon gave way to "modernization," but for the first few years that I remember of haying, we loaded the loose hay from the field into a wagon with side racks to contain the load. The wagon was hitched behind the loader, and the tractor towed both across the field. The loader was an upright trough-like affair on wheels that picked up the windrowed hay and conveyed it up into the wagon. This operation, of course, required more than one person: a tractor driver, and one or two in the wagon with pitchforks to distribute the hay evenly in the load.

Riding back to the barn on top of the load was sheer pleasure, sprawling in the sweet smelling hay as the wagon lurched in the hill road ruts like a schooner on heavy seas.

At the barn, the wagon was positioned under the gaping haymow door on the end of the building at the peak of the roof. The tractor was unhooked from the wagon and backed up to the corner of the barn where a heavy rope was attached to the drawbar. This rope ran through a series of pulleys routed up into the peak of the barn, and arranged in such a way as to hoist the hay into the mow with a sort of grapple fork type apparatus. This fork was set into the hay load, and the tractor was driven away from the barn, pulling the rope and hoisting the hay. I was about seven years old when this became my first solo tractor driving assignment, and I felt like a king! Up went a portion of the load, and when it reached the peak, the fork struck and attached to a trolley mechanism and then rolled on a track suspended from the roof peak the entire length of the mow. My brother was usually the one to set the fork, and he had control of a trip rope rigged to the fork. When it reached the desired spot in the mow, the trip rope was jerked and the hay was released into the mow. The fork was then pulled back down to the load and the operation was repeated until the entire wagonload was in the barn. Just as on the wagon during the loading, someone – usually Dad – had to be in the mow with a pitchfork to distribute the hay in even layers, to make room for the maximum amount of hay in the limited space. When he came down from there, he would be drenched in sweat, and hay chaff clinging to every part of him made him look like some furry green creature.

Then it was back to the field for another load.

It was about 1957 or '58 when our neighbors, the Sordahl brothers, got their first hay baler. Their place was four times the size of ours, and they were quite the progressive farmers. Ernest, the younger brother, had recently returned from Army duty. He was a bull moose – way over six feet tall and solid muscle – a stronger man I did not know. Size wise, Otto was just the opposite – small and wiry, but he, too, had the strength of two men his size. They were always wonderful neighbors, and I think because my Dad was considerably older, they were always eager to help him in any way they could.

That year, between their first and second crops, they brought their new baler to our place and baled a large portion of our hay, too. It was a rather noisy contraption – one with its own gasoline engine. The racket sent the cattle scurrying off to the farthest corner of the farm away from the field where we were working. But noisy or not, Dad seemed quite pleased with the way those square bales stacked on the wagon and in the barn, and the fewer trips required to the field to haul in the crop.

Well, that did it. The next summer, a *Leon Implement* flatbed truck showed up at our place one day with our brand new, bright red Massey Ferguson hay baler. From then on, the haying operation changed for us. It was still a lot of hard work, but it seemed to go a little faster. And since our experience with the bales the previous year, we already knew how feeding the cattle during the winter had become a much simpler task.

Haying time brings back some pleasant memories. It never seemed to fail that at least once or twice during the summer, threatening weather would catch us with a bunch of hay bales left in the field to haul in. Dad always took pride in getting his hay in the barn without it getting rained on, so he pushed us a little harder and we'd work a little longer if he suspected a rain cloud to let loose.

On one occasion that I recall, we had been working very hard to "beat the weather." The longest strip on top of the hill was all baled and ready to come in, but the forecast was rain that night, and as hot and humid as it had been all day, and the way the sky looked in the west, the approaching storm was likely to reach us before nightfall.

After the third or fourth load, Mom was at the barn waiting for us to return with the next load. "I've got dinner all ready for you," she said. "Come and eat." She was aware of the weather situation, and we suspected that was why there seemed to be a little excitement in her voice.

Dad dug out his pocket watch and saw that it was already past noon. For just a moment he studied the western sky with that look of concern, and then he peered at Ralph and me. Our stomachs were growling, and I'm sure his was, too. We knew how important it was to get all the hay in before the rain, but just the same, we would have mutinied had he rejected the offering.

When we reached the front yard, we realized why Mom had called us to dinner with such enthusiasm. There, in the pleasant shade of the big pines, a fabulous meal awaited us spread on the picnic table! Platters filled with fried chicken, potato salad, baked beans, sweet corn, a mountain of fresh homemade bread, a big bowl of applesauce, and a pitcher of cold milk.

Our mid-day fatigue seemed to melt away. We dashed to the washbasin at the cistern to get rid of the field dust from our hands and faces, and then hurriedly found a place at the picnic table to enjoy the wonderful feast.

That little variation in the everyday routine seemed to give us all a booster of fresh energy. When we had finished eating, we went right back to the hay hauling, because we didn't dare take our usual little siesta for fear of the approaching weather. And that sudden spurt of new energy got all the hay in the barn. As we neared the bottom of the hill road with the final load of bales, the first sprinkles fell from the ominous charcoal clouds. Ralph gave the Allis a little more gas, making a run for the shed as if it were the last lap of a championship race. Just as the back of the wagon pulled through the shed doors, the heavens opened up with a cloudburst, and it poured rain for nearly an hour.

Dad wore a big grin, proud of our efforts in winning the battle. I climbed up on the hay load with thoughts of a well-deserved nap while we waited out the storm. I knew Dad was thankful, and I can imagine Mom was smiling, too, thinking that perhaps the picnic under the pines had been an encouraging bit of help in our never-ending war with nature and the elements.

A Summer Storm

Over the tops of the hills hung a vast thunderstorm, purple as King Cole's robe, with shafts of pale sunlight streaking down through it. The storm moved down on us like the hordes of Genghis Khan, and there always seemed to be a number of crows, screeching and swooping, as if they were leading it about. (Crows are related to ravens. In Norse mythology, Odin had two ravens, Munin and Hugin, who flew about the world gathering news for him. Ravens, too, are fond of battlefields and have flown over them like black, ragged flags. They are often associated with the "dark side," so, should we, then, beware of gathering ravens? Or, in this case, crows?)

I attribute my strange sort of attraction to thunderstorms to a time when it seemed a perfectly natural thing to be out on the lawn with my dad and older brother, perhaps perched on top of the picnic table or leaning on the fence posts at the edge of the back yard, to watch the approach of a threatening storm. And the greater the severity according to the predictions, and the darker the clouds, the more intrigue it seemed to instill. Just an ordinary, non-eventful rain shower would simply drive everyone indoors with little excitement, but a fierce, rip roaring thunderstorm – now, that was something worth staying out to watch! When I was quite young, I was never certain what the others expected to see – perhaps a funnel cloud dropping out of the deep purple sky, or maybe Dorothy and Toto and a strange house might plop onto our yard. Sometimes Mom would hover at the screen door and scold us for staying outside. But nonetheless, we sat there, watchful of the storm's progress, eyeing the ominous, churning clouds and spikes of lightning, listening to the crackle of thunder that seemed closer every second, until the wind made it almost necessary to lean in order to remain upright, and the first drops of rain stung our faces as we retreated to the porch. From there we watched the gusts of wind spin eddies of dust in the gravel driveway and rippled a few loose shingles on the woodshed. Then the mischievous little zephyrs flapped the curtains through the open windows, a warning to my mother who dashed through the house pulling out the screens and slamming down the windows.

Then the storm was upon us with walls of rain sweeping over the hills. There was the rumbling, booming thunder and the breathless, scalding flashes of lightning, the hiss of the rain and the howl of the wind – the tremendous noise and fury drowned out all other sounds, and there was a misty, steamy quality in the air.

Sometimes, these splendid storms passed quickly as they went raging off toward other hills. Behind them, the sun came out again, and the newly washed world glittered all around.

But on rare occasions, the rainfall lingered for days on end until the earth could absorb no more. At first, pools of water started to appear in the fields, the barnyard, the pastures, and even on our lawn. Rivulets began trickling down from the hillsides that grew to gushing streams, expanding the pools to lakes. Gradually, the ditches and dry runs filled with coffee-brown water that swirled and eddied and foamed as it tumbled over the rocks, making its hasty trip to the main creek bed. All this runoff from thousands of acres of hills upstream from our farm swelled the creek to overflowing, and soon, nearly our entire valley was covered with one big silent mass of rapidly moving brown flood. Cattle would sometimes be stranded on a hillside on the wrong side of the creek, and there was nothing we could do but wait for the flood to recede. Often these surprise summer and autumn floods came during the night, and they were more threatening and deadly than the springtime torrents that were always expected and prepared for.

Our house was situated only fifty feet from the creek bank. More than once the floodwaters flowed within just inches from its wall facing the stream, threatening our safety. And on a couple of occasions, the rising water imposed a more serious threat, making it necessary for us to flee to higher ground! When it appeared that the flood might invade our home, Dad announced to the family to get dressed. (It was usually in the middle of the night.) We gathered a few blankets and pillows, Mom made a pot of coffee and sandwiches, and we spent the remainder of the night in the car on top of the hill overlooking our not-so-peaceful little valley. As lightning illuminated the landscape, it was like looking down on the Mississippi

River, and all the farm buildings appeared as boats, completely surrounded by water.

We were safe up there on that hill, but we never knew what we would find at next dawn, when, perhaps we could return to our house. I would fall asleep on the back seat of the car, wondering if anything would be left at all, and even at the very young age I was at the time, I recognized Mom and Dad's concern. I'm sure they didn't sleep much on those nights.

I awoke in the morning, only to learn that Dad and my brother had walked back down the hill to survey the situation at the first light of day. The cows were safely in the barn for the morning milking, and they wouldn't be too eager to venture back out into flooded pastures. On the opposite hill, I could see the forlorn, stranded young livestock huddled, seeking a little protection from the rain under trees. The flood had not yet begun to recede, and did not until nearly noon that day, so the Dodge remained on the hill as our emergency shelter, and there we stayed. It was like camping out, but we would have all preferred better conditions.

The rain had all but stopped during the early morning hours, and by mid-morning, we could see the flood shrinking a little. Then, just before noon, Dad returned to the car and said the bridge at the driveway was no longer under water, and that it might be safe to go back to the house. What a relief.

The Dodge splashed through the puddles left in the driveway to the garage, and then we splashed through the puddles getting back to the house. Fortunately, the floodwater had not raised high enough to enter the house, but we could see the water line left behind by the ebbing current – it had been dangerously close. We were lucky that only the cellar had partially filled with water, and we could all breathe a little easier knowing that we still had a home.

Snooker, our cocker spaniel had spent the night on a stack of hay in the barn, and the hens in the chicken coop were frantically clucking their disgust with the dreadful conditions, but all were safe and accounted for. By mid-afternoon, Dad managed to take some dry hay across the creek with the tractor and wagon to the stranded young stock.

Our farm was seriously threatened that night, but as creatures of survival, we emerged unharmed. God had spared us, our animals, and our domain from catastrophe, and we were all quite grateful.

The Forest

Those huge pines stood about the yard – I'd guess over fifty feet tall – comforting, protecting, utterly over-shadowing the house below with its upstairs dormer window and white slate siding. The crickets sang in the evening, and you could hear the gentle wind in the tops of those pines, and then it whisked off to rustle the leaves in the trees on the hills beyond.

All the forested hills surrounding our farm were my favorite places to explore. The trees absorbed all the manmade noises, and the air was soft and cool, and the sunlight filtering through the canopy had a glow of friendliness found nowhere else.

In the stillness, all the delightful forest sounds could be heard – the hushing of the wind through the upper branches; a squirrel scurrying about; a woodpecker drumming on a dry tree limb, and then his wings drumming the still air as he flitted to another tree; even the distinct, neat sound that a twig makes when it falls to the earth. If you listen carefully when you walk in the forest, you can almost hear each leaf stir in the breeze, and the forest's aroma of wildflowers and sap and ferns can revitalize anyone's senses.

To the west of our farm lay a vast wooded area that continued on for miles over the hills and through the valleys. It was there that I ventured – at first with my older brother, before I learned a good sense of direction.

But eventually, I could navigate the hills and woods on my own, only getting temporarily lost a time or two, until a familiar landmark was located, directing me back on track.

Sometimes we would make it an all-day journey. We'd pack a lunch of peanut butter, bologna, or cheese sandwiches wrapped in waxed paper and stuffed into a brown paper bag, along with a few cookies, and maybe some graham crackers. We never needed to carry water, because there were many springs in those hills, and we knew just where to find them. Out of those springs bubbled the clearest, purest, most deliciously sparkling water that I have ever put to my lips – we were never left thirsty on any of those hikes.

I'd carry the brown paper sack with the food, and Ralph carried a fishing pole. If we had decided to make an overnight stay, he toted a hatchet and a roll of blankets tied up with a rope, and my bag of food was just a little bigger. We didn't need much – just the bare essentials.

Somewhere along the way through the woods, we would stop for a rest. I remember sitting against a tree trunk in the dim light, and seeing the slanted shafts of sunlight falling through the canopy of leaves like the light through stained glass church windows. Orange and black Monarch butterflies danced about on the still air among the trees, and vines hung from the high branches in long, graceful loops. On the ground was a carpet of dead leaves, and all around were the green-leafed saplings and shrubs poking up through, and occasionally a little patch of wild white lilies and bright yellow buttercups. Now and then the sunrays would catch a clump of ferns just right, and it glowed like a fountain of fire. Later in the year, we would return to this place to pick blackberries from the lavish bushes lining the western edge of this forest where the land dropped away into the valley.

Compared to a city street, the forest seemed so quiet. Yet, there were many voices. Overhead, the leaves murmured in the wind and insects hummed. Not far away, a squirrel chattered, and startlingly close, a songbird warbled a tune. Off in the distance, something created a disturbance in the dry leaves. I jumped, thinking it sounded like enough noise to be made by a bear, but Big Brother assured me there were no bears in these woods. He was sure it was probably a grouse, or maybe a fox chasing a rabbit.

I was becoming quite aware of the life in the forest, and I wondered how many pairs of eyes were watching us. But it seemed that most of the creatures cared little that we were there, and every time I visited the forest, I felt more at home, one creature among this vast fraternity.

After our little rest stop, we shortly came to the edge of the woods at the top of a steep hill. We were overlooking a stream coursing along the hill on the opposite side of a green, lush valley. Long before we reached this point, we had passed the boundaries of our farm, but this was the same stream that passed across our farm, although here, downstream, it was somewhat larger. Worn into the steep hill was a pathway, and I would guess that it was used mostly by the animals of the forest trekking to and from the valley stream – I think man would have followed a less difficult angle to ascend that hill.

The floor of this little pocket of the valley nestled among those remote hills was rather marshy, especially along the creek. But there was high and dry ground, too, and because we had been here before – Ralph, many times – we knew the way across to the dry spots. Now, as you might guess, knowing your way across a marsh is important, as it is not difficult to find yourself sinking neck-deep into a slimy mud hole, so cleverly hidden under a growth of marsh grass. This place wasn't so particularly treacherous, but it did require a little caution.

On the other side of the creek, accessible by way of rocks at a little stretch of rapids, the hillside carpeted with plush, green pasture grass sloped gently away, with only a scattering of oaks and hickory trees. About fifty yards above the rapids, and about a hundred feet back from the creek bank, stood the decaying remains of a small, tumbled down log house. This had once been a homestead, perhaps the original site of the buildings of our neighbor's farm, and in such a remote spot, it is not surprising that the dwelling place had been moved to its present, more accessible location. But what a beautiful little valley this was!

Ralph caught some nice trout that day, while I chased frogs and watched the ducks among the cattails. Late in the afternoon, we constructed a makeshift lean-to tent with sticks and a blanket, and then, in the last bit of golden sunlight, we went off downstream a little ways to watch the industrious beavers, busy at work maintaining a dam that contained an enormous pool of deep water. These animals are quite entertaining, however, their workday begins at sunset, and you'll rarely find them out on a bright, sunny day.

Our timing was perfect, for not only did we see the beavers, but not long after we settled down on the bank, acting like statues, a mama raccoon and her four kits came to the shallow creek just below the beaver dam. She was apparently teaching the youngsters to fish, and I'm not sure whether they dined on trout or frog legs that night, but they definitely captured something they thought was quite delicious.

When it was too dark for us to see the beavers or the raccoons, Ralph and I headed back to our camp, built a little fire, roasted hot dogs, and curled up in our blankets. We listened to the hooting owls, and I tried to count the stars.

Some people are afraid of the forest, images cast in their minds by mythology and fairy tales where the woods were the domain of ogres, elves, witches, dragons, giants and demons. But I felt safer there than anywhere else, as to me, it became the place of adventure and romance – the home of Robin Hood and the hunting ground of Hiawatha.

If any great calamity were to overrun the nation, I think I would seek a forest for its safety and comfort.

Living in the country offers rewards that city dwellers seldom consider. Co-existing with nature is one of those rewards. I couldn't begin to count the different species of wildlife that inhabited the valley and the hills on and around our farm. I remember hiking through the woods as a youngster, and never a single journey would be without sighting a dozen or more varieties of birds. And there were always squirrels, chipmunks, rabbits, raccoon, opossum, and even deer. I had all my favorite spots to watch the animals, and because I was such a frequent visitor, I thought the animals were beginning to trust me, and they made very little effort to scurry off and hide when I was around. Owls, though, were often heard but rarely seen, as most of their activity is at night. Their keen eyesight and silent flight makes them good nighttime hunters. Their fluffy, soft feathers insulate them from the heat and cold, and make them appear much larger than they really are. The hoo-hoo-hooooaw call of the Great Horned owl or the screeching cry of the Barn owl can be a spooky sound on a dark night.

Things to Entertain

Mine is perhaps the last generation to experience the "non-high-tech" era. We grew up in a transition period when the modern world was still coming of age. The depression was over. World War II was over. Although there was still a hot spot that challenged world peace, I was yet too young to be concerned about the Korean conflict, or even aware. Rural life, then, seemed uncomplicated and easy to enjoy, even though there was no TV, computers, or video games to occupy the time.

By the time I was old enough to understand my limited environment, our farmhouse had been endowed with electricity. Of course, that didn't mean much to me then, as none of my activities required the use of electrical power. In fact, it would be several years until electricity became of any importance to me. What was important to me then was "Cuddles," my butterscotch yellow Teddy Bear that never left my sight, and a set of wooden blocks with the alphabet carved and painted on them in bright colors. I couldn't spell yet, but I loved those blocks.

I don't recall having many other toys (although there probably were some) until Christmas at about age four or five. My sister, Rachel, (who we called "Ricky") had gone to Williston, North Dakota to work as a telephone operator after she graduated from high school. That year, because she could not be at home, a package arrived in the mail from her just before Christmas that contained gifts for the family.

45

I'll always remember the excitement on Christmas Eve when the package was opened. That night I became, perhaps, one of the littlest Texas Rangers in history. My present from "Ricky" was a hand-tooled, two-holster gun belt, complete with a pair of shiny, pint-sized six-shooters, and if that weren't enough, there was a pair of very fancy high-healed cowboy boots, too!

I'm not sure why those things held any significance to me at that time, because we did not yet own a TV that could have provided the cowboy and Indian influence on a youngster my age, although I might have been introduced to Gene or Roy at a movie theater by then. The only other reason the boots and guns excited me so much may have been due to the Lone Ranger and Tonto episodes I was probably hearing on the radio by then. At any rate, I refused to relinquish the gun belt or the boots that night when bedtime rolled around. I'm told in later years that I slept with them on. I wonder if Cuddles was jealous.

Within a short time, I began to grow into that "industrious" age, as most little boys do, and building things seemed to occupy my time most frequently. Nothing in the house was safe from my ingenuity in making use of almost anything as construction materials. Chairs, sofa cushions, pillows, blankets – anything I could handle or move. And of course, if there happened to be an empty cardboard box left over from a trip to the grocery store that Mom or Dad didn't put to immediate use, it was more than likely to become some part of my construction materials repertoire.

Undoubtedly, Mom and Dad recognized my obsessions

of building things. I remember some of my favorite Christmas toys after that were the Lincoln Logs, American Logs, (Lincoln Logs were round; American Logs were square.) and the red plastic bricks. (They were probably the forerunner of "Legos.") With all those construction toys to occupy my time, even though now everything was built in miniature, the rest of the house remained intact.

Then came the most extravagant Christmas present I can recall, as far as toys were concerned. It was given jointly to my brother and me, and at last we were thrust into the high-tech, electrical age with the Lionel train set. It was one of the larger scale models with a heavy replica steam engine that would actually puff smoke from the stack. It pulled several realistic freight cars – box, flat, tanker, cattle, hopper, and caboose. The set came with enough straight and curved track sections to make a six-foot by four-foot oval, or a figure eight. We never had a place to set it up permanently, so it was assembled and disassembled hundreds of times over the years – usually on the living room floor. Eventually, we acquired more track sections, and our railroad grew. And naturally, the most common commodities hauled were the Lincoln and American Logs and the red plastic bricks for building a town on the far side of the living room.

That electric train was still operational when I was a teen-ager, and I'm sure that it is probably now amidst some proud hobbyist's collection of antique toys. I wonder if toys made today are that durable.

Weather permitting summertime outdoor activities didn't usually involve many toys, except for maybe ball and bat, the Radio Flyer wagon, or a bicycle. Living on a farm on a gravel road, there were no sidewalks or pavement on which to roller skate, and no one yet had even thought of the idea of a skateboard. Because I spent so much of my childhood alone (my brother was nearly six years older, so we had very little in common once he became a teen-ager) playtime required a certain degree of improvising: a ball thrown up onto the granary roof always came rolling back, and the roof never once complained that I threw the ball too high, too low, or too hard. The creek was a great place for sailing the homemade wooden boats, and the hills provided wonderful propulsion for a thrilling ride in the coaster wagon.

Of the few store-bought toys suitable for outdoor use, the most memorable for me were the balsa wood glider planes. Although they weren't the most durable of toys, they always were a thrill – when I could convince Mom to part with the twenty-nine cents to buy one for me. And on special occasions – maybe a birthday – she might even splurge sixty-nine cents for one with landing gear, a propeller and a rubber band motor! Their simplicity was what made them a great toy. All the pieces were pre-cut, and were easily assembled by sliding the wings and rudder into slots in the fuselage. In a matter of minutes you had an airplane ready for take-off. Most of them had adjustable wing position to allow for straight-line, long distance flights, or all sorts of acrobatic maneuvers such as loop-de-loops or spiral bank turns.

The only poor quality of these fantastic flyers was that the material they were made of – thin balsa wood – was somewhat fragile, and after a few crash landings, or a sudden gust of wind that carried the glider off course smashing it into a power pole, shed wall, or tree trunk, the components splintered into kindling, ending a great day of aviation. More than once, the high branches of the huge white pines on our yard snatched my aircraft. Occasionally, the wind might shake it loose, sending it plummeting down in a devastating tailspin, but often it was never to be seen again. I think the birds probably found them there, picked them to pieces, and used the soft wood for nest building.

A Creek, a Bridge, and a Boat

My desire to build things had progressed to the outdoors, too. Aside from the usual, crude forts and huts that little boys build in the country, my construction projects involved several attempts at bridges. A marvelous little creek coursed its way through the valley that divided our farm in halves. Another dry creek bed followed another smaller valley that branched off to the north side of the farm, and a deep gully that originated on the neighbor's land to the south never had any regular, steady flow of water, but they did, however, carry tremendous volumes during spring thaws and periods of heavy rainfall. But during the normal summer season they were empty, and the creek width varied between ten and thirty feet, and it was easily forded with tractor and machinery at a couple of crossings where the creek bottom was mostly small stones and gravel, and the water shallow. I remember there being a bridge at one of those crossings, but it had been carried away by a flood and was never replaced.

To say the least, the geographic layout of our farm provided numerous bridge building opportunities, although they were a bit more imposing than a boy might imagine. But my older brother and sister had told me of a footbridge they once built across the southern gully years previous, and if they could do it, so could I.

But I had my sights set on bridging the water-filled creek. To me, that seemed more useful than spanning a dry gulch in a part of our farm that was largely wasteland. On one side of the gully, the trees there were mostly box elder, and the hillside was so steep and grassless, that even the cows didn't want to go there. On the other side, though, was a pleasant, grassy knoll adorned with maples and white birch, and it had been a favorite playground for years. I had named it "Birch Hill." (How's that for originality?) But it was easily accessible by crossing the rocky creek at its foot and climbing the cow paths up to the top without passing through no-man's land. Why build a bridge there?

After several unsuccessful attempts to span the water, I finally decided that timbers long enough required falling trees a little larger than I could handle. I wasn't yet old enough to operate a chain saw, nor were there any trees of that proper size and length near enough to the creek, anyway.

It was time to reconsider other options. I searched the farm for another useful bridge location, but I found nothing but more of the same difficulty already encountered.

I surveyed the dry gulch. Maybe reaching Birch Hill via no-man's land from atop the hill road at the edge of the hayfield wouldn't be so bad, after all. Farther up the hill, the ravine narrowed and wasn't quite the deep Grand Canyon gap of where my siblings had stretched across the first bridge. That place was now much wider as a result of flood erosion over the years, and presented the timber length complication again. To overcome that obstacle, I chose a narrower, less challenging spot, and it just happened to be up around the bend where a cow path ended at both sides of the gully. Perfect!

And so the bridge project began. I immediately went to work chopping down a couple of tall, straight birch trees in the woods farther up the hill – nobody would miss them from way up there! After two or three days, this pint-sized lumberjack had struggled with the timbers to finally get them to the construction site. As I recall, I used the light-weight block and tackle that Dad always kept hanging in the granary to snake them most of the way, and to get them in place across the ditch. And of course, a young boy doesn't always employ the most precise measuring methods, so naturally the timbers were short by a foot for the intended location. However, by pivoting one end and relocating the Birch Hill end by a few feet, they were long enough, the only problem being a rather large oak tree just a few feet from the bank. But there was just enough room to get by, so the project went forth.

With the timbers finally in place, I was ready for the next step. On the other side of the farm, a little ways up the valley with the dry creek bed, Dad kept a pile of scrap lumber and fence posts, and it was there where I would procure the materials for the bridge deck. Another few days of intense labor – cutting the boards to length with a hand saw, and no doubt there were a few blisters that came out of that part of the project. Transportation to the bridge site via Radio Flyer coaster wagon meant many trips, as there was a creek to ford and a hill to climb, so the loads couldn't be too big. But at last, all the boards were nailed in place, and I finally had a way to get my wagon up on Birch Hill. Although it didn't pass over a body of water as I had originally planned it would, I had constructed a bridge, and I was rather proud of my accomplishment. And that project had kept me entertained for at least a couple of weeks.

The creek still remained a barrier that I was determined to conquer. If I was unable to successfully build a bridge across it, then I must create a craft to sail upon it. I had made many little versions of various types of watercraft complete with wind sails, and even with rubber band motors that propelled a tiny paddlewheel. Navigation in miniature on this great waterway was a lot  of fun, and I couldn't see anything stopping me from building a craft large enough to carry me in it. Surprise, surprise!

I soon learned that Tom Sawyer and Huck Finn must have weighed absolutely nothing, or else their raft was much heftier than what would fit in my little stream. I concluded that it was the latter. An old barn door floated quite nicely, and convinced that it would be the ideal creek craft, wide and flat, I equipped myself with a pole for propulsion and prepared for the journey from the base of Birch Hill to the woods at the far edge of our farm, a distance of at least a hundred and fifty yards. This was, perhaps, the longest stretch of open "navigable" water on the entire farm without rocks and rapids, and the concept of rafting that distance excited me. I stepped aboard, and my Titanic was quickly at the bottom under my weight. Luckily, the water was only two feet deep.

"Surely," I thought, "there must be a solution to this navigational dilemma." Then it occurred to me that the boats I had seen at the river all had sides. So, clearly the answer was that I needed sides, too. I vaguely remembered a time when we – my siblings and me – used to float in an old cattle-watering tank on a stretch of creek farther downstream near the house. It was between two big bends where the water was quite deep and wide before the DNR came in with a bulldozer and straightened out one of the bends. But our boat of yesteryear – that cow tank – had been lost to a flood, and it was rather doubtful that Dad would allow me to use his present tank for sailing on the high seas.

A boat with sides. I did not know how to build a boat with sides. But I remembered a contraption used for mixing up cement – a wooden tub-like thing that, for all practical purposes, was shaped kind of like a boat. I located my prospective new vessel out behind the granary among a few other discarded and forgotten pieces of junk. It was about three feet wide, five feet long, and the sides were about eight inches. I thought it would make a dandy boat.

The Radio Flyer quickly went into service as a boat transport, and with some difficulty in keeping that clumsy cement tub balanced on the wagon over some rather rough terrain, I managed to arrive at the launch site at the foot of Birch Hill late that afternoon.

This would assuredly be a success, because this vessel had sides! I maneuvered the wagon to the water's edge and let the cement mixing tub slide into the water. So far, so good. Because I could kneel or sit in this boat, this time I had a short length of board that I would use as a paddle. I glanced to the west to see the sun still high in the sky. There was enough time for a trip to the line fence and back before I had to fetch the cows for the evening milking.

Everything was all set for the maiden voyage up the creek. I carefully stepped into the cement mixer, knelt down, and pushed the craft away from the bank, ready to start paddling. I quickly learned two things about using a discarded cement mixing tub for a boat: first, it has the dynamics of a brick, as the only movement I could accomplish with the paddle was to make it spin without any forward progress; and second, that it was not exactly a water-tight vessel. After less than a minute afloat, it filled with water, and the Queen Mary was on the bottom. I guess you could say this gave new meaning to the saying "up a creek without a paddle."

Discouraged, and sitting in two feet of muddy creek water, I decided that maybe it was time to get the cows from the pasture, after all.

Radio and TV

As far back as I can remember, the radio was an important part of our family's everyday life. Of course, the broadcasts meant little to me at first – they were merely extra voices coming out of that wooden box with dials and knobs, talking about things I didn't understand. But then there would be music, and I did enjoy that.

Then language became meaningful, and little by little, I started to realize how that radio connected us with the outside world. Mom and Dad listened intently to news programs, and afterwards they sometimes talked about the events described in the broadcast. And Dad paid particular attention to weather reports – he'd often plan his farming activities according to the information he heard. And often, we would hear him grumbling a day or two later if it rained on his newly mowed hay after the weatherman had assured him of clear skies. But likely as not, he'd be listening and planning again the next day.

As I recall, there was scarcely a day – except maybe Sunday – that our noon dinner table wasn't the sounding board for the farm market news announcing the most current prices paid for corn, oats, wheat, hogs, and any other commodities that interested farmers wanted to hear. Then there was the local news, and the day just wasn't complete without Paul Harvey delivering his comments about the day's events. He'd always end his program with a humorous ditty, and his unique sign-off: "I'm Paul

Harvey"... long pause... "Good-day!" I often wonder how many people across the country, at those moments, held their breath during that little pause, and tried to anticipate and imitate Mr. Harvey's unique "Good-day!" like I did.

Come evening, the chores done and the supper dishes cleared off the table, we all gathered in the living room where the radio was tuned in to Amos and Andy, George Burns and Gracie Allen, Bob Hope, Jack Benny, Red Skelton, Edgar Bergen and Charlie McCarthy, or Fibber McGee and Molly. I still remember those great sound effects – like Fibber McGee opening a closet door and all that junk tumbling out! There was something marvelously special about the whinnies from the Lone Ranger's horse, Silver, and his thundering hoof beats. There was something intriguing and spine tingling in the suspenseful footsteps during a mystery from the Shadow. And Jack Benny's violin... WELL!

We'd sing along with the Hit Parade, and sometimes Mom would give a few basic dance lessons during the Guy Lombardo Show. We would occasionally hold our noses in response to some of the amateur performances on Arthur Godfrey's Talent Scouts, and we'd laugh ourselves into tears with the antics of Minnie Pearl and Grandpa Jones on Grand Ol' Opry.

And then something quite magical happened – television! A TV station in La Crosse, WKBT, had started broadcasting on a limited schedule late in 1954. Of course, at that time there weren't TV sets readily available in local stores, yet, and if they were available at all, I'm sure they were quite expensive. But my aunt and uncle who lived in

Chicago had been watching TV shows for quite some time, there in the big city, and somehow word came to Mom and Dad that they were getting a new TV set, and we could get their old one. So, off they went in the Dodge one day, to retrieve our first television from Chicago. My brother and I had to stay at home to take care of the chores and milk the cows – a trip to Chicago and back was at least a two-day voyage, even in a Dodge.

In wild anticipation, we waited for their return. It was August, so there was no school yet, and we were home when the two-tone gray Dodge pulled into the driveway. It seemed almost like Christmas, although I had never seen TV, and I didn't really know what to expect. Dad and Ralph carried it carefully from the trunk of the car and sat it on a table in the living room. It looked like a large radio with an eight-inch round glass window, that, when plugged in and turned on eventually produced a black and white array of... snow! And the sound was nothing more than a loud hiss. I'm not sure where the antenna that they had mounted on top of a clothesline pole came from – probably Chicago, too – but it obviously needed adjusting. Dad went out to the back yard and slowly changed the position of the V-shaped arrangement of rods with little results of anything resembling a picture appearing on the screen. Because we lived in a valley, he determined that the antenna had to be up higher, so it was moved to the house roof, and attached to the chimney.

That project was finally finished after the evening chores, and after Dad climbed the ladder to the roof several times, with Mom yelling to him through an open window to let him know when a picture and sound appeared, we had TV! As I recall, the first television programs I saw that night on the tiny screen were the *Lawrence Welk Show* and *The Hit Parade.*

Channel 8 from La Crosse was the only station we could receive, so our choice of programming was quite limited for some time. But it didn't really matter so much. We were still entertained with the shows that were available... game shows such as *I've Got a Secret* with Gary Moore, and Groucho Marx on *What's My Line?* "Say the secret word and win a prize," he'd tell the contestants, and we'd always wait for that stupid-looking duck to drop down with a little sign in its beak bearing the secret word. Corny, but entertaining. Then there were the comedy shows... *I Love Lucy*, and *Jackie Gleason*, among several others, and I was thrilled to finally see the masked man – The Lone Ranger, and Tonto, and Silver – the voices and sound effects of which I had only heard on radio.

We had that TV for about a year, or so, and it was, once again, passed on to some other relatives when one with a larger screen replaced it in our living room. In the years to come, several attempts to relocate the antenna in order to receive other stations rendered less than perfect results, but determined Dad managed to accomplish the reception of Channel 10 from Rochester, Minnesota and Channel 13 from Eau Claire by mounting the antenna high in a pine tree, up on the hill beside the house. I think that's where it stayed for as long as we lived on the farm.

But the coming of TV did not entirely replace the radio. Paul Harvey still bid us a "Good-day" every noon, and Dad still tuned in the weather reports every morning to plan his day, and although the radio version of the Lone Ranger was no longer a part of my evening entertainment, the radio still provided plenty of music, and maybe a baseball game now and then. At some point in time, there was a small portable radio added to the barn. Dad had heard somewhere that cows liked music, and they would give more milk if a polka band serenaded them during milking time. Well, maybe they did like the polkas, but I doubt if the bucket would have been any fuller because of the secret word duck.

A Coaster Wagon and a Bicycle

There were two important vehicles intertwined in my youth, and I remember their origins quite clearly. As the youngest child of the family, I was often the recipient of hand-me-downs – everything from boots to caps, and a few toys here and there. But one advantage to all this was that although some of the things had managed to survive, by the time they got to me, they were pretty well worn out, and in dire need of replacement.

My dad was quite conscientious about maintaining for me such things as the old coaster wagon that had survived my sister and my brother, and had served my light duty purposes, too, for a while. But as I got a little older and found more challenging tasks for that wagon, its rusty old carcass simply fell apart under the strain, and Dad was no longer able to make the necessary repairs.

So, around my birthday – I was probably about six – Dad took me to town one Saturday on a feed mill mission, and after a hamburger and chocolate milk at Borgen's Café, we ventured across the street to Flugstad's Hardware Store where I thought he would buy some nails or fence wire or maybe a new axe handle – it was getting close to the time for wood splitting. But instead of going to the nail bins in the back of the store, he led me down the isle on the squeaky wood floor to where there were several different coaster wagon models on display. "Okay... pick out the one you want," he told me. I was thunderstruck. I could hardly contain myself. I was about to become the proud owner of a brand new wagon!

I might point out here that not all "little red wagons" were red; I picked out a blue one. And just like all other little boys, my wagon went with me everywhere that I could manage to take it on the farm. It made a great downhill racecar, a covered wagon to cross the prairies, (Yes, I did fashion bows with very flexible willow branches and draped feed sacks over them!) a stagecoach to deliver the mail, and a dandy truck for all those building projects. It was quite useful, too, for all the practical chores: it carried apples from the orchard on the north hill, vegetables from the garden, wood from the woodshed to the porch, and even buckets of feed from the granary to the chicken coop. My dad could have made no better investment in any other birthday present.

Unless, of course, I consider what came along a few years later. I had learned to ride a bicycle at about the age of eight with the usual get-a-push-from-Dad-and-crash-twenty-feet-away routine that went on for quite some time. Perhaps it would have gone better if the bike hadn't been so big and so heavy, for I was just a little guy. That bike had originally been my sister's, and was handed down to my brother, and then finally to me. Now, when my brother inherited the monster, it was a girl's bike, and a boy could not be caught dead riding a girl's bike. So, Dad took it to a welding shop in town and had a bar welded into the frame, and viola – a boy's bike!

Just how old that bike was, I do not know, but the name on it was Hiawatha, and I think Hiawatha may have been the first to ride it. It had umpteen coats of different colored paint – everything from John Deere green to Allis

Chalmers orange – and it weighed a ton. It was rather shaky when I started riding it, and after two or three years more, it had seen better days, but it was still getting me to school and home again.

I arrived at home after school with that old clunker on my tenth birthday expecting to find a neat pair of cowboy boots that I had seen in town and hinted that my birthday was just around the corner. But there were no boots. Instead, my dad was in front of the granary tightening the last few bolts after assembling a shiny new bicycle... my shiny new bicycle... a bright red *Huffy* with 26-inch whitewall tires and chrome fenders! Oh, boy!

"Happy Birthday," he said.

"Gee! Thanks, Dad!"

And after a few minor adjustments of the seat and handlebars, I was off like the wind, touring the neighborhood for the next two hours. I guess Dad didn't expect me to help with all the chores that day. After all... it was my birthday, and a new bike couldn't just sit there looking pretty.

Birthday Bike...Chrome fenders and whitewall tires...Oh! What a joy!

Memories of a River

Rivers are remarkable in that they belong largely to the children. Fishermen and children retain a love of rivers – others regard them only as barriers to cross or sources of spring floods. They build bridges over them and dams to stop them.

But children enjoy them. I remember viewing the Mississippi River with awe at a very early age. Even then, I think I understood its greatness. I put my bare feet into the cold water and squealed with ecstasy. I stared for hours into the swirl of water looking for the excitement of fish. I threw stones into the rougher parts, delighting in the "plop" I heard over the waves splashing against the shore rocks; or if the river was smooth, I skimmed flat stones across the surface. I floated sticks, leaves and pieces of paper out into the water, launching the great ships of the world. I stood by that mighty river that gleamed like silver, its banks gilded with wild iris, and I dreamed of great travels through strange lands to the ocean.

When I was just a small child, Sunday picnics for the family during the summer months were a common practice. After church, Mom would pack up a big basket of sandwiches, potato salad, baked beans, cookies, cakes, a giant jug of Kool-Aid, and all sorts of goodies. Then we'd all pile into the car and Dad would drive us to one of our favorite getaways to enjoy the day. Our destinations varied: sometimes it was just a spot along the creek bank in Timber Coulee; sometimes he took us to the lake at Hatfield, or to the picnic grounds at Wildcat Mountain. But more often, we spent the day somewhere along the banks of the Mississippi River – our favorite spot being a little county park on a hillside overlooking the river somewhere between Stoddard and Genoa. From there I could view the pleasure boats zipping along, but my favorite sight was that of the big barges slowly plowing their way up or down the river.

My brother and I would play the usual boy games of catch or tag after the great picnic lunch spread out on a blanket. (As I recall, there were no picnic tables in that park, because there wasn't a level spot to put one.) But our attention would always be drawn to the river when a towboat and barges passed by. This must have sparked a memory in Mom – it was then that she told us of her younger days when she came to Genoa as the new teacher in a country school there, and of course, she was not yet familiar with the ways of the river people.

That was before the locks and dams were in place on the Mississippi, and the boats were powered by steam engines and paddlewheels. It was customary in those days for the residents along the river to greet the riverboats that passed by, often by ringing a dinner bell on their yards facing the river. The pilots of the steamboats would answer the greeting with cheery tooting of their whistles.

People along the river loved the big boats, and generally would stop whatever they were doing to watch and wave. And this custom stayed very much in effect, even at the school. The first time Mom's pupils raced out of the school to watch and wave to a whistling steamboat, she had tried desperately to coax them back to class, but nothing held priority over viewing that boat until it was out of sight. From that point on, whenever a steamboat whistle sounded and the children ran out of the school, she knew all she could do was to join them. And she did.

And so my fascination with the river and the big boats was nothing new – it was an ages-old pastime that seemed to come naturally to me. Now, when I watch the silent, great river, and the swifts and the gulls skimming its surface hunting insects, and I see a tow of barges slowly pass by, I think of that little park on the hillside and of our Sunday picnics, and I can return home very much younger.

Empire Builder

Train Ride to Chicago

What could be more exciting to a young boy than to take a trip to a big city on the train? When I was about five or six years old, there probably wasn't much that could top that. So, when Dad suggested that Mom and I should take the train to Chicago to visit my Aunt Dolly and Uncle Sam and Cousins Robert and Ralph that summer, I could hardly contain myself. It would be the first vacation trip I would take part in – that I could remember – that involved traveling farther than to a county park down by the river for a Sunday picnic; it would become a memory that would last a lifetime.

I remember, quite clearly, standing with Mom on the

platform at the railroad depot beneath Granddad's Bluff in La Crosse waiting for the Empire Builder to arrive. Dad was there, too, to see us off. I had been at the depot before, to meet my Aunt (who we were going to visit on this trip) when she came to visit us on the farm. But this time, being there seemed more meaningful, because I was going to board that train. And when I heard the train horn blow, long before it was within sight, my excitement escalated to something unimaginable. I had seen this train before, so I knew what to expect, but this time, the massive, silver locomotives and the string of silver passenger cars with their blue stripes running their full length seemed more majestic, and as I looked up at the car windows and saw faces looking back at me, I knew that in a short time I would be one of those faces, and the excitement became nearly overwhelming.

As the train rolled slowly to a stop, a uniformed man jumped from an open doorway in the side of the train and placed a little step stool on the ground in front of the doorway. He tipped his hat and offered pleasant farewells to the people coming out, and frequently helped a disembarking passenger with a suitcase.

Then it was our turn. The porter welcomed us aboard, and then we passed through several cars until Mom finally pointed me into a set of seats that faced each other. By that time, the train was already rolling, and quite some distance from the station. I was disappointed that I had not been one of the faces looking down at the people on the platform, but as I would find out later, I would have many more opportunities for that before the day was over.

We zoomed out across the countryside, and soon I was

staring out the window at a familiar sight – the Mississippi River. Somewhere along the line, Mom pointed out the opposite windows to the park in the hillside where our family came often for Sunday picnics, and before long, the train was slowing to a stop in one of the Mississippi River towns. Finally I was one of the faces in the window!

I had been a little frightened at first by the porters who passed through the car and always stopped to ask my mom if there was anything we needed. I had never seen people with black skin before. But Mom assured me that there was nothing to be afraid of, and they did appear to be always smiling and quite friendly, so I soon got over my fear of them. And come lunchtime, I was eager to follow the porter to the dining car. There we had a bowl of soup and ham sandwiches, and as a special treat, Mom ordered a dish of ice cream for me. So far, riding on the train was a great experience.

When we arrived at Chicago late that afternoon, I was very much afraid that we would be lost forever. The station was enormous, and quite intimidating to a little boy. But luckily, Mom had been there before, and she seemed to know where to go. And just as she was hoping, Aunt Dolly and Uncle Sam were waiting for us at the entrance. After all the hugging and kissing was out of the way, we found their car in the parking lot, and drove what seemed to be just as far as we had come on the train through the biggest city I had ever visited, with taller buildings than I had ever imagined, and more cars, trucks and buses than I had ever seen, coming and going in every direction. We finally arrived at their house in the suburbs.

My cousins, Robert and Ralph, were both considerably

older than me, but that didn't stop us from having a wonderful time. Living in the city, they had a lot of neat toys and games to play with, and I guess that was probably necessary – they didn't have a granary or a hayloft, or a creek or a woods – just a concrete sidewalk and a fenced-in yard that was not much bigger than our chicken coop on the farm. Now I understood why they were always so excited to come stay at our farm for a week every summer.

Just down the block from my aunt's house was a neighborhood grocery store – the "market" they called it – and I was pretty amazed with the number of trips to that store my cousins made for a jar of tomato sauce, or a gallon of milk, or a box of crackers. At home, we went to the grocery store once a week and came home with several bags and boxes of groceries. I couldn't remember a single time that we'd ever made a special trip to town for just one jar of pickles.

During our stay in Chicago, the kinfolk were quite the tour guides and activity directors. Although it seemed like we spent a lot of time just getting somewhere in that big city, I saw places and things that most kids my age had never dreamed of seeing. We spent one afternoon at Lincoln Park Zoo, and another at a wonderful amusement park where my cousins took me on roller coasters and all sorts of other rides. And one night, they took us to the top of the Sears Tower, the world's tallest building at 110 stories. I think the elevator went faster than the Empire Builder.

Another night, my cousins took me to a movie theater. I don't recall what the movie was, but I remember the surprise I had when we came out. At home, when our family would come out of a theater late at night, the streets were quiet and nearly deserted, and the only people moving about were the people leaving the theater. But there, in Chicago, the streets were just as busy and noisy when we came out as when we went in. I wondered if the people in the Windy City ever went to sleep!

I went home feeling that my cousins were two mighty lucky boys, living in a place with so much excitement and so many things to see. But now I realize all the things they couldn't do: they couldn't swing on a rope in the hay mow, or go fishing in the creek in summer, or go skiing or sledding in the winter, or just go tramping in the woods on a bright September day. As much as I had enjoyed my visit to the big city, I was glad to call that little farm in Wisconsin my home.

The "Elephant Tree"

This old oak tree was near the top of a hill overlooking our house in the valley. We were always curious about how it  came to grow in such an unusual form, suspecting that it had, perhaps, been damaged by a storm. We always called it the "Elephant Tree," because its shape reminded us of that animal. However, in my recent research, I have discovered that we should have called it the "Indian Tree." When this tree was a young sapling, it was bent into this long lasting marker by the Native people who used marker trees like this one to point out trails and natural features, just as we use road signs today. Considering its location and the direction in which it points, it may have shown the way to a flowing spring.

Night

There are so many things to remember about the night – like the swaying yellow light of a lantern on the way to the barn, and the old witch clouds scurrying across the face of the moon on a late October night while the wind whispered in the pines – there was a certain gracefulness that the daytime lacked.

Nighttime in the country was always a mysterious thing. I like to remember those soft, mid-summer evenings when the darkness seemed to crawl into our valley and wrap around everything like a velvet cloak. It flowed gently and if I held my hand out, I could sense and feel it. The sounds of the night were like the notes from an organ swimming in the thick air. A calf bawled in the barn while the frogs serenaded from the creek. Somewhere in the distance, a hound bayed, and in the woods behind the house a couple of owls hooted their messages back and forth, unconcerned with the squeaks and chirps from the dozens of hungry bats darting about in the night air.

The dew settled in the grass as if an invisible rain had

fallen from a clear sky. Fences and bushes made shadowy, mysterious patterns, animated by the blinking and winking of ten thousand fireflies. And the fragrance from the lilacs was almost intoxicating.

It was usually this time of night – when the chores were done and supper eaten – that a family of one of my school friends, or maybe some relatives, or perhaps the neighbors from down the road would stop by for a social visit. The men folk would gravitate to the porch or the front lawn and discuss cows, weather, the corn crop, and the milk prices they were getting from the creamery, while the women gossiped or traded recipes in the kitchen. If there were other kids, we'd be off into the night, climbing trees, investigating the creek banks, or looking in on the new baby calves in the barn. But I loved the drowsy sound of conversation on the porch in the night, and the squeak of an old rocker added the perfect background to a symphony that sounded as good as fresh coffee smells.

Before the night could end, everyone gathered around the kitchen table for a late night "lunch." The grownups had their coffee, and the kids drank gallons of Kool-aid. There was always a big plate of bologna and cheese sandwiches, several varieties of homemade cookies, and cake – there was always cake – sometimes with gooey frosting, or sometimes with ice cream. That was the part of the evening that every kid looked forward to.

Although the night often yielded the soft, velvet touch of a spring breeze, it sometimes was cold and harsh. I remember so well one particular night just after the sun dipped behind the hill to the west. Dad kept staring into the sky toward the northeast. A lurid, orange glow faded one instant, and flared the next. It could only be one thing: someone not too distant had a major fire.

Dad backed the car out of the garage. Mom got in the front seat with him, and my brother and I got in the back.

We turned north at the Jacobson corner; the glow seemed to be the brightest in that direction. When we topped the Jacobson hill, it seemed obvious the fire was on the Elefson place. Their farm buildings were near the intersection of the Jacobson road and the North road. (Those weren't the official names for the roads – just designations made by the local farmers.)

Cars, trucks, and people lined the roadway all along the Elefson property in view of the barn that was engulfed in flames. Dad drove past the house, turned onto the North road and parked. When we first arrived, the shape of the barn was still recognizable, but before long the walls deteriorated and the roof began to collapse, and it soon was nothing more than a blazing heap of rubble. Dad had gotten out of the car and was standing by the fence next to the road. A couple of other men that he knew walked up to him and they began talking. "Well, they got all the cows out," I heard one of the men say. "But some of the young stock was still in there."

The blaze was so hot and so intense; the firefighters could do little but protect the rest of the buildings nearby. We could see the Elefson family standing near the house, helpless, with many of their closer neighbors and friends by their side, offering support at such a dismal time. The Elefson children, who were older than me, didn't attend the same school as I did, so I never knew them very well, but we had been to their house a time or two for the neighborly nighttime social visits and coffee, and I knew the family to be some very wonderful people. I had often wondered why our families didn't socialize more than we did. I guess they were just far enough away to be in "another neighborhood." At any rate, I felt bad for them and their devastating loss.

We drove back home in the chill of a black night. It had been a night of excitement, but the kind of excitement that left a numbing feeling inside. For quite some time after, when we would take that road into town, it was always depressing to see that blackened pile of burned hay and rubble – the only remains of the barn where I had participated in hide and seek games in its haymow. The Elefsons had lost an important part of their livelihood, and for me, a small part of my childhood went up in smoke that night, too.

It was a big relief when the debris was cleared away, and a new barn started taking shape at the Elefson place.

Fall Harvest

When I was growing up, harvest time meant more than just bringing in the grain crops. It was a time that seemed to unite the whole neighborhood, and as I recall, threshing day was always one of the highlights of the year. Everyone pitched in as neighbors helped neighbors to accomplish the job, and to ensure that all the farmers in the area got their grain under a roof while weather permitted. All of it was done with shared equipment, shared labor, and a shared sense of community.

August marked the beginning of the grain harvest season, when the oat fields transformed from a sea of verdant green to pale yellow, and then to radiant gold. But prior to threshing day, much preparation was needed. About a week or so before the threshing machine came, we cut the golden ripe oats with a reaper, or binder as it was commonly called – a machine that mowed and tied the oat straw into neat bundles. (This was another implement originally designed to be horse-drawn, and modified for tractor power.) Every year it seemed the reaper required a certain amount of repair and maintenance. There was always a cracked or broken board to be replaced in the reel. The cutting bar always needed at least one or two new sickle blades, and of course, all the blades needed sharpening. The canvas conveyor belt always seemed to mysteriously develop rips and holes that needed mending. And then there was the usual bolt tightening, chain adjusting, greasing and oiling. (All the working mechanisms were driven by flat, square-linked chains, one of which transferred the power from a large gear attached to the "bull wheel," a big, wide, steel lugged wheel that carried most of the weight of the machine over the field.)

Besides getting the machinery ready, the bins in the granary needed cleaning to accept the fresh new crop of oats. During the year, as the bins had gradually emptied of the previous year's crop, the vacated space seemed to attract all sorts of things – a catch-all for tools and supplies and odds and ends – and as long as we were at it, why not clean out and straighten up the entire building? As I recall, one year we really did a housecleaning in the granary, and we hauled away several wagonloads of what we considered junk. (Today it would be called antiques.) All that junk was buried, when later that summer Burl Burns came with his bulldozer and rebuilt the hill road up the to the north fields.

When everything was ready, Dad hitched the perfectly operating binder to the Allis Chalmers tractor, and with me riding in the seat on the binder (where the driver sat when the machine was powered by horses) off we went up the new hill road to start cutting the grain. Then the bundles were stacked in shocks in the field to complete the drying process.

In our neighborhood, Clifford Thompson owned the threshing machine. He would coordinate a schedule to include all the neighbors on a "threshing tour," coming to each farm for the harvest. The other farmers came with at least one tractor and wagon to haul the grain bundles from the fields to the machine, and when it was their day for the threshing machine, the favor was returned. Everyone worked together as a team.

"The threshing machine is coming tomorrow." That announcement was electrifying to a youngster. It meant that, first, the steam engine with threshing machine in tow would come chugging and hissing and rumbling down our gravel road. That was almost as good as a circus parade. I'd sit on the porch steps from early dawn, waiting to hear the heralding steam whistle sound from up the valley, proclaiming that threshing day on our farm was about to begin. Soon, all the neighboring farmers would start to arrive, and they would assist Clifford in setting up the threshing machine for operation. Sometimes he had to dig little holes in the ground for the machine's wheels to sit in, in order to get that huge contraption level. Then it was a matter of expertly positioning the engine so the long drive belt was perfectly aligned between the pulley on the threshing machine and the drive pulley on the engine. All this time, our farm was a beehive of activity, as some of the neighbors drove their tractors and wagons to the fields to start loading the grain bundles. By the time they returned, the thresher was ready to run.

That machine, to a little boy, seemed a fascinating monster! It appeared as big as a barn, arrayed with pulleys and belts and gears and chains. It whooshed and rumbled and whirred – all at the same time, as the men pitched the bundles of grain onto the conveyor that fed it into to the mouth of the monster. On one side, the grain that had been separated from the straw and cleaned of the chaff spouted out from a chute, where one man stood and filled gunnysacks, or shoveled the grain into a wagon. At the other end, a long, large diameter pipe extended out and spewed the golden straw onto the stack that grew as the day wore on.

I was too little during those first recollections of threshing day to take part in the activities, but it was great fun to watch – I didn't want to miss a single minute. As I grew a little older, I learned how to drive the tractor, and I could actually be a member of the threshing crew, piloting a tractor and wagon in the field while the men pitched the grain bundles into the wagon. It was such an honor!

Mom was responsible, too, for one of the grandest parts of threshing day – the noon meal. She, like all the other farmers' wives on their threshing day, arose early in the morning to start preparing a feast for a dozen or more men who would certainly be hungry by noon! Sometimes, one of the other women in the neighborhood helped with the task, and no finer banquet could be found anywhere on the whole planet. The main course was roast beef or meatballs or ham or meatloaf or fried chicken, mountains of mashed potatoes, gravy, tons of vegetables from the garden, fresh homemade bread, and pitchers of ice-cold milk. Usually, the day before, several pies were baked, along with cakes and cookies, and the threshing day dinner table was laden with enough food for a small army. No one left hungry.

After a short rest in the shade of our huge pines, (and one more cup of coffee) everyone returned to the threshing again, hauling and pitching, shoveling and stacking. At regular intervals during the day, a wagonload of oats went to the granary to be shoveled into the bins, and I can still remember the smile on my dad's face as he watched a good yielding crop fill those bins to overflowing.

At day's end, the threshing was done, and all the neighbors headed for home with their tractors and wagons, for it was milking time. There was a high degree of satisfaction felt by all, and no one regretted his time donated to his neighbor's task, as he knew his turn was coming soon. Even though it had been a day of hard work, it had also been a day of social gathering, when all toiled shoulder-to-shoulder, building a strong community.

The passing of the steam engine was a sad blow to the enjoyment of the harvest season. Somehow the magic of the day was diminished when a gasoline-engine tractor powered the big threshing machine. It still whirred and rumbled and whooshed, but there seemed to be something missing without the chug-chug-chug of the steam engine and its whistle's cheery song.

The date hand-written on the back of the original indicates that I was about 14 years old when this snapshot was taken, however, I do not recall where it was taken. This engine is very much like the one that came to our farm and powered the threshing machine similar to the one below during grain harvest.

WINTER

Eskimo Joe, Snooker, & Dad's 1952 Dodge

Long Johns

As a youngster, I can remember hearing the grownups talking of the "Cold War." Although I would eventually learn all about the politically stressful world situation, it seemed that we waged our own cold war – it was us against the cold! From early November until early April the battle with Old Man Winter and the emergencies he created was the normal state of affairs for the folks who lived in the country.

During those days the sight of someone walking outside gave a good idea of what it meant to be prepared for the weather. If his teeth were chattering while he attempted to keep his coat wrapped tightly about him, it was clearly understood that he wasn't wearing winter underwear. Those who wish to make comic fun of "long johns" should have had an exposure to our winter weather conditions.

Now there was more to this matter of long underwear than you might expect. There has probably always been a difference of opinions regarding the fleece-lined, flannel, or all-wool versions. My Dad was the woolen follower, but I thought that wool was scratchy and uncomfortable, so I preferred the flannel. Of course, I don't recall my Dad ever complaining of it being too cold for him to be out to do the necessary work on the farm.

There was also the argument about the merits of separate shirts and pants as opposed to the combination "union suit." Some men preferred the shirt and drawers, while others stuck with the one-piecers. The women were inclined, if they were the frugal type, to suggest the shirt and drawers, because when a pair of drawers wore out, they were simpler and cheaper to replace than the combination.

In Roehl's Clothing Store, there was a counter toward the back where all the boy's underwear was stacked. My Mom was quite the thorough shopper. She would search and sort through the stacks until she found what she thought to be the right size. I didn't mind any of this unless there were other people near and Mom insisted that I stand up straight while she held the long johns up to my waist checking for proper fit. If they weren't at least six inches too long, they went back in the pile and the search continued. Mom seemed to know my growth rate, and she refused to spend money on long johns that I would outgrow before the end of winter.

And naturally, there were always questions of which brand was the best. "Mr. Roehl," Mom would ask, "you must know which of these is the best. They're getting so expensive that a person has to get the best value."

Mr. Roehl would clear his throat and look helplessly to the front of the store where the men were pretending not to listen. "Well, they're all good. Some like this one, and some swear by that one." He delivered the statement triumphantly in hope that he had settled the matter.

Then Mom would throw out another question that seemed to require a more definitive answer: "Do you think the heavier one is worth the extra money?"

Knowing that we were a farm family, Mr. Roehl recited the best possible answer: "Well, a boy out on the farm should probably have the heavyweight."

That seemed to finish the discussion.

The Wood Stove

My recollections of life on the farm would not be complete without mention of our main defense against the cold – the wood stove, and of course, the fuel to keep it burning. Every time I hear the furnace rumble to life now, I can be thankful, for there was a time that keeping warm meant a lot of hard work. On the other hand, there was something about that old bulky hunk of iron that made our country home the most pleasant and comforting place to be on a chilly winter night.

Our parlor wood heater was not of the "pot belly" variety, but rather a more fashionable-looking apparatus that seemed to blend in with the furniture. About five feet tall, three feet wide and deep, square but with nicely-rounded corners, and enameled with a sort of wood-grain brown, shiny finish, it sat on a shiny black, four-legged base that gave it five or six inches of clearance from the floor. There were two doors on the front side: the lower door provided access to the ash pan and contained the air vents to control the draft, and the upper door opened the firebox for inserting the wood chunks and lighting the fire. On the back, an open water tank gently steamed a little humidity into the air.

As a boy I was very fond of that stove. It had character and a certain dignity. By the time I had grown a little older, I hated it, although my hatred was confined to spring and autumn when it had to be moved. There was an unwritten law that stated this Buddha-like creation had to be taken out to the granary for the summer months, and then returned to the living room in the fall when the weather started getting a little nippy.

When the first signs of frost appeared, Mom would casually suggest that "maybe we should bring in the wood stove pretty soon." Dad would usually ignore that first hint, but when the living room furniture was rearranged to accommodate the stove, he knew he couldn't put it off any longer. Mom wanted the stove in... now!

It always happened to be a warm day when the dreaded task of moving the stove into the house finally arrived, making it seem a bit ironic, but nevertheless, we knew it had to be done. Before I was old enough and big enough to be of much help with the iron monster, Dad and my older brother, Ralph, couldn't quite manage the task without a little extra help. Dad would usually recruit one of the neighbor men for some assistance – Otto and Ernest Sordahl were always willing to come on a moment's notice if Dad needed help with something.

It was strange how friendly and warm that stove looked in the winter sitting in the living room, and how intimidating it seemed now. The thing weighed a ton, or so it seemed, and no matter where you grabbed to lift, there was a sharp edge. Getting through the wide granary door and into the pickup truck was not a problem, but after the fifty-yard ride across the front lawn, negotiating that beast into the house was another matter. The maneuver required a certain amount of manipulation, and invariably, half-way onto the porch, the removable grate on the top would slide off and land on someone's foot, and the firebox door that ordinarily opened only with effort, now came open by itself with ease and slammed someone's elbow or hand in the process.

After the usual jiggling, tilting, turning, and trial of every possible angle, it was decided that the house door should be removed from its hinges. Fact was we had never gotten that stove through without taking the door from its hinges, and we also had never been able to resist trying.

Once into the room, Mom called out navigational instructions, as it was rather difficult to see exactly where you were going with a ton of wood stove pressed against your face. She would have in place the metal-clad board that the stove sat on to protect the floor. Positioning was never absolutely certain, but the guesswork always seemed to suffice. It had to – once that stove was put down, it didn't move until next spring.

Next came the matching and aligning of the stovepipes. I am quite certain that the devil invented stovepipes just to try man's patience. The sections were either too long or too short, or the elbows not quite the right angle, but somehow, it always went together. And on that first chilly night with a fire blazing, the pipes pinging and popping, and the friendly warmth radiating across the room, we began to like the monster again. When the wind rattled the windowpanes and whistled its icy tunes out among the white pines in the yard, there was no greater comfort than to sit close to that stove roasting stocking feet, while the cocker spaniel slept contentedly on a rug behind it. Even now, on a blustery winter night, I sort of miss that old stove.

The thought of that stove and cold winter mornings, though, instills in me a bit of sympathy for my father. It was a feeling I didn't have as a boy; however, experience has taught me that he must have endured some miserable first waking moments nearly every day during the cold winter months. I can picture his bare feet dancing on the cold floor while quickly getting dressed. Sometimes I would hear the commotion as a dresser drawer squawked when he slid it open in search of a pair of socks, and clunked shut again. Then I would hear his footsteps on the squeaky stairs down to the kitchen, the door onto the porch opening, and the familiar rattle of kindling being gathered from a bucket. The fire lighting ritual then involved the tearing and crumpling of some old newspaper that was placed in the bottom of the firebox, with the kindling piled over it, only after shaking down the old ashes into the ash pan beneath the firebox. That was a noisy process in itself. The paper was ignited with a match, and if done properly, within a few minutes a couple of chunks of larger wood could be laid in on top of the blazing kindling. During the whole procedure, the iron hinges squealed and squawked, and the door clanked open and shut several times, sending metallic reverberations throughout the entire house.

My brother and I occupied the bedroom directly over the living room. If we weren't already awake, the racket downstairs was probably intended to get us stirring. Of course, we were playing possum, huddled in the warmth of our bed, hoping the heat from the stove would have improved the conditions a bit by the time Mom finally rousted us out to get our chores done and ready for school.

Keeping the wood box on the porch full was a job automatically entrusted to me every fall. As long as there was no snow, my Radio Flyer wagon made the task a little easier. The wood shed stood about fifty yards from the house, and for a young boy that was a long distance to tote armfuls of split wood. When the snow made for difficult wagon navigation, out came the sled. It didn't seem to work as well as the wagon and wouldn't haul quite as big a load, but it still saved a few trips over carrying the wood by hand. I wasn't particularly fond of the job, especially if deep snow prevented the use of either the wagon or the sled. But every morning and every evening, it had to be done whether I liked it or not.

As miserable as it may have seemed at times, I still miss the comfort of that old stove.

A Trip to the Feed Mill

When Dad bought his first pickup truck, some things changed for me, too. Before that time, he would load gunnysacks filled with corn and oats onto a farm wagon, and pull the wagon with the tractor to the feed mill in town. During the summer, I was often allowed to ride with him, but in the winter, during the school year, that didn't happen, even if it was on a Saturday. I'd guess he didn't want to expose me to the discomfort of the four-mile ride on a hay wagon that didn't offer much protection from the elements.

But a pickup truck changed all that. When a trip to the mill occurred on a Saturday, a warm truck cab was a luxury that I'm sure even Dad enjoyed.

The loading began as soon as the chores were done and we had eaten breakfast. First, Dad would back the truck up to the corncrib and shovel the ear corn into the box. When the box was almost level full with corn, the truck would be moved to the granary door, where we shoveled oats on top of the corn. The oats sifted down through the ear corn and settled at the bottom. By the time we got to town with the load, you could barely tell there were any oats at all. Once the grain was loaded, Dad tied a bunch of empty feed sacks in a bundle and tossed the bundle on top of the load. We were ready to go to the mill.

If the roads were particularly icy, Dad would have already put the tire chains on the truck, which meant slower traveling, but if it were just an "average" winter day, the heavy load in the truck usually provided for adequate traction.

When we arrived at Ben Logan's Feed Mill, there were always at least one or two trucks in line ahead of us. It never took a long time, but to me it seemed like a lifetime. Then it finally came our turn to unload. I was usually deposited in the office where a kindly secretary always had a candy dish on the desk. After a few minutes, the truck would be moved around to the loading dock, and I would go out there to watch the mill men fill our sacks with feed from a chute, tie each one shut with a piece of twine, and load them back into the truck. The mill was a noisy place, but fascinating.

By then, it was close to dinnertime. (To us, then, the noon meal was called "dinner" and "supper" was eaten in the evening.) Depending on what other errands were to be incorporated in this trip to town, or which eatery tickled Dad's fancy that day, he would strategically park the truck within reasonable walking distance to the stores we would visit, and then head either to Norma's Café on West State Street next to the drug store and Goettel's Meat Market, or maybe to Dinty's or Borgen's on Main Street, or sometimes we'd go to Jeffson's Café on East State. It didn't really matter to me – I liked them all, and having a hamburger and chocolate milk at any restaurant was a treat.

Mom usually handed over a short list of grocery or household items she needed before we embarked on the trip to the mill; however, this was never intended to be a major grocery purchase. That was Mom's duty. To fulfill this list, we had several choices of stores: there was Goettel's Meat Market, or the Clover Farm Store, or Storbakken's, or Balsrud's, or there was the Southside Grocery on the way out of town if we happened to forget something. They all had the penny candy bins, and Dad usually let me get a dime's worth of something. As I recall, the chocolate haystacks at Storbakken's were my favorite. Yes, those trips to the feed mill had their rewards.

The Big Snow

When we went to bed it was cold, with gusty winds that seemed to scatter the clouds around in a majestic sort of disarray. Stars pinpricked the black sky. Earlier in the day there had been a swirling series of dry, fluffy snow flurries but they didn't amount to much.

Dad had been listening to the wind, and we noticed him several times tapping on the glass of his beloved barometer that hung on the kitchen wall, just inside the door leading to the porch. Then he'd go out on the porch for another look at the sky, and through the open door we could hear the northern zephyr howling over the hills that surrounded our little valley.

"Barometer's falling," he'd say, back in the kitchen again. "We're due for a change tonight... probably snow." Then he would load up the wood stove and partially close the chimney damper to slow the burning and preserve fire for as long as possible through the night, and then like clockwork he would plod up the stairs to bed.

The anticipation of snow carried double meaning for a couple of young boys on the farm. It meant the beginning of a season of skiing, sledding, snow forts and snowball fights, and all the fun stuff kids do in the snow. But it also meant shoveling and added inconvenience to all the outdoor chores. For me it meant the probable end of hauling firewood to the house with the wagon. But the thought of snow still captured a bit of excitement in us, and we ran to the window to check the current weather status.

"He's usually right," Mom would say as she set aside

her mending project, "and there will probably be snow on the ground tomorrow." Then she'd glance at the clock, or catch one of us yawning. "You two. It's late. Off to bed." Mom was usually the one to enforce the bedtime curfew.

Up the stairs we tramped, shucking clothes on the way and then plunging under the quilts and blankets. With only foreheads and noses exposed, we listened to the wind gusts brushing the side of the house for a while before we fell asleep. At some point during the night, I awoke to utter silence. Not even the old house was creaking. It almost seemed as if the whole world had come to a standstill. I could have gone to the window and scratched away some of the frost to see the change taking place, but it was too cozy to leave the comfort of that warm bed.

In the morning we discovered the magical transformation that had come about sometime during the night. Just as Dad had predicted, the ugly brown and gray autumn lay under that magnificent carpet of pure, clean white. And the snow was still coming down – we could hardly see to the barn, great drifts of white everywhere.

There was always something fascinating about that first big snowfall. After losing their colorful autumn leaves, the naked trees now had white strips on trunks and branches. Every twig held a dab of the stuff. The snow hid from view the rubble left behind from the garden harvest and put comical caps on all the fence posts. It even gave the cistern pump just outside the kitchen window a fat new look. And wouldn't you know? A stupid old hen that had wandered off the day before now came wading through the drifts from her hiding place in the roadside weeds seeking the shelter of the chicken coop.

Can there be any greater fun for a boy than to tramp around making tracks in the fresh snow? And of course we had to check the snow to see if it could be packed into a snowball. This was the one time when you could get away with lobbing a snowball at Dad as he finished the chores around the barn. There seemed to be a strange sort of lightheartedness that came with a snowstorm like that one.

My brother and I trudged off through the snow to school. Our one-room school was nearly a mile and a half away from the farm by way of the road, but less than a mile if you knew the short cut over the pasture and fields, across the creek and through the woods. Rarely did I follow the road, except in the fall and spring when the weather permitted riding a bicycle.

Our coats, caps, mittens and scarves were arranged with the others around the furnace vents for drying, and the whole school had that humid, woolly smell. Everyone sported rosy cheeks, and hair all askew after pulling off a stocking cap, but everyone was happy and in good spirits. It was the first big snowfall of the season, and that excited kids.

By early afternoon, the snow had not let up, and just before the scheduled recess, a man appeared at the door. It was the father of a little girl in school. He had come to escort his daughter home, and told the teacher that it might be wise to send the other children home as well. After looking out the front door, the teacher wisely took the advice and dismissed classes for the day. In no time at all we were dressed and headed in all our separate ways.

The early dismissal came none too soon. By the time

we reached home, the drifts were nearly non-negotiable for a little guy like me, and the biting wind seemed to slice through wet clothes like a razor. We were mighty glad to be home.

It was a good day to get the chores done early. Even Dad and Ralph finished the milking earlier than usual, and we all pitched in and carried an extra supply of firewood into the porch. Mom had gone into baking mode that morning, so there was plenty of fresh bread and biscuits waiting on the table for supper.

Even though the storm raged on outside, we were all together in the safety and comfort of our modest home. Mom made popcorn later that night, and she didn't make Ralph and me go to bed early because we were quite certain there would be no school the next day.

The storm roared on all the next day. Chores were the only essential work. The rest of the time we could read or just be lazy any way we wanted. Dad lay on the living room couch, read the newspaper, and napped. I helped Mom make peanut butter cookies, and Ralph spent most of the day upstairs in our bedroom working on one of his model ships. Sometime during the afternoon we all came together again from our individual interests, and Mom and Dad, each with a hot cup of coffee, and Ralph and I, each with a glass of Kool-aid, enjoyed a plateful of fresh, still warm-from-the-oven homemade cookies. The fires were stoked and there was time to look at all the Kodak pictures and relive the adventures of a vacation trip we had taken to the South Dakota Badlands long before I was old enough to remember it.

Another day rendered much the same activity, except

Mom baked more bread and I couldn't be of much help, so I built a cabin with the Lincoln Logs.

The storm finally broke that day and the township snowplow opened our road. The mailman came, and we had to go to school the next day. There was a bittersweet feeling of loneliness because the storm had finally ended. In that isolation, we had found the warmth of togetherness that resides in every family, but is sometimes neglected in the happenings of everyday life.

My new Christmas sled! This snapshot was taken in front of the one room country school, South Natwick, where I received my first seven years of education. Wintertime noon hours and recesses were usually spent on sleds and skis.

Skating

Too few youngsters today get to enjoy the delights of skating that the previous generations experienced. Going to the local artificial rink can't measure up to shouldering skates and scoop shovel and trudging down the lane, across the pasture until you came to the big, wide bend in the creek. Removing the snow from our skating "rink" required much more shoveling than clearing a path from the house to the barn, but somehow it didn't seem nearly as much work.

When I was a little older and going to the school in town, I made a lot of new friends from "other neighborhoods," and during the winter I would often be invited to their Friday night skating parties. I'd ride with them on their school bus to Mike's place near Bloomingdale, and after the farm chores were done, we'd head to their "big bend" about a half a mile up the road. There'd be no less than twenty kids show up. Some would shovel to clear the ice, while some built a blazing bonfire. Then there was sound of skate blades singing on the ice that was, perhaps, not exactly smooth, and happy shouts echoed across the valley as the fire crackled and splashed its flickering light against the hillside.

For just a little while on those nights, the angels watching must have envied the earth people.

ABOUT THE AUTHOR

Joel Lovstad spent his childhood on a small dairy farm in west central Wisconsin not far from the Mississippi River. In later years he went off to college in nearby La Crosse. After many years of working and living in various big cities, he always longed for the life of the country. Now in retirement, he resides in a small central Wisconsin village.

33878618R00062

Made in the USA
Middletown, DE
30 July 2016